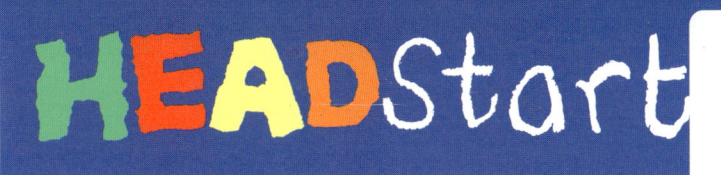

Number skills

Shirley Clarke & Barry Silsby

Illustrated by Trevor Dunton

BROCKHAMPTON PRESS
LONDON

NOTES FOR PARENTS

This book aims to help your child:

- feel confident about being a mathematician;
- remember and understand number facts, like times tables and number bonds, and solve maths problems;
- use and understand concepts like negative numbers and division;
- understand the patterns in our number system;
- develop mental skills.

You can help your child get the most out of this book by:

- *talking* about the activities, without 'telling' your child how to do them. Encourage your child to think of different ways of working things out.
- *not stopping* your child using his or her fingers to count, or of using what may seem to be long, drawn out ways of working things out. When children are confident with their own methods, they can be shown quicker ways of doing things.
- *letting your child control the pace* of working through the book. Too many pages in one go may put your child off.
- *giving lots of praise and encouragement*. Children get better at subjects they believe they are good at.

Pages 4–5   Feed the birds

Division is a difficult concept, so children need activities like this, where sharing is done physically on a 'one for you, one for you' basis. Encourage your child to share out the raisins equally, by cutting them in two or more pieces if necessary, which will lead to talking about fractions.

Pages 6–7   The lollipop machine
Apart from showing combinations for adding, this activity can be used to help develop skills of logical and systematic ordering. Look at the answers to see how a systematic approach helps to find all the ways to make the number.

Pages 8–9   Vital statistics
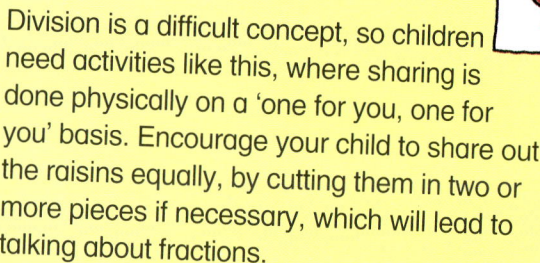
This is an opportunity to help your child measure accurately. Make sure the measuring begins at zero on the tape measure. If you think your child is ready, help him or her to count the millimetres for even more accuracy.

Pages 12–13   Adder bingo

Playing this time and time again will help your child learn number bonds off by heart. Notice there are more sevens than any other number on the boards, because there are more ways of making seven than any other number using two dice.

Pages 10–11 Broken calculator

This is similar to the lollipops activity. All the numbers after seven can be made using threes and fours, although you may not think so initially!
(For example, 17 = 4 + 4 + 3 + 3 + 3 and 25 = 4 + 4 + 4 + 4 + 3 + 3 + 3.)

Pages 14–15 New prices

This activity helps your child with rounding up or down, and with learning the convention of using decimal notation when writing money amounts.

Pages 16–17 Tables game

The idea of this activity is that children use the tables during the game, which should help them make more sense of them. You could introduce the word 'multiple' as well (for example, 'You've got a 3. Is 18 a multiple of 3? Let's have a look at the 3 times table.').

Pages 18–19 Maths factory

This is an algebra activity - looking at function machines. The child needs to focus on what has happened to change the numbers.

Pages 20–21 Number trivia

This activity develops mental skills. Don't stop your child using fingers, however, as this is an important stage in children's mathematical development.

Pages 22–23 Giant jumps
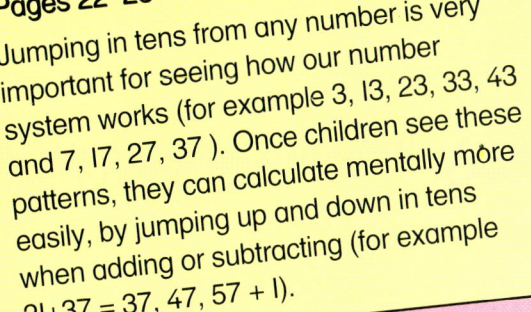
Jumping in tens from any number is very important for seeing how our number system works (for example 3, 13, 23, 33, 43 and 7, 17, 27, 37). Once children see these patterns, they can calculate mentally more easily, by jumping up and down in tens when adding or subtracting (for example 21+37 = 37, 47, 57 + 1).

Pages 24–25 Negative numbers

This activity focuses on an understanding of whether an outcome will be positive or negative. Because of this, using a calculator is suggested for checking. Make sure your child recognises the minus sign on the calculator (sometimes it is on the far side of the display).

Pages 26–27 Number square patterns

This activity uses a 1 to 100 square as a resource for finding out more about patterns in numbers.

Pages 28–29 Number jumble

Ordering numbers is difficult, but very useful in helping your child understand place value. It is easy to miss numbers out, so encourage your child to take time over the task. Ideally, the numbers would be on real cards, so that they could be ordered physically.

Pages 30–31 Games and puzzles

These are fun activities. Children could be encouraged to make up their own puzzles.

Feed the birds

Ask if you can have 20 raisins, sultanas or something similar.

Share them equally between the birds. How many each?

Start again and share out 12 raisins between the birds. How many each?

Clue
You might need to cut the raisins!

Now try these:

Share out 8 raisins. How many each?

Share out 4 raisins. How many each?

Share out 10 raisins. How many each?

Share out 16 raisins. How many each?

Share out 14 raisins. How many each?

Share out 9 raisins. How many each?

Answers on page 32.

The lollipop machine

How many ways can you put 8p into the machine?

One way has been done for you. Can you find some other ways?

Write them on the coins below.

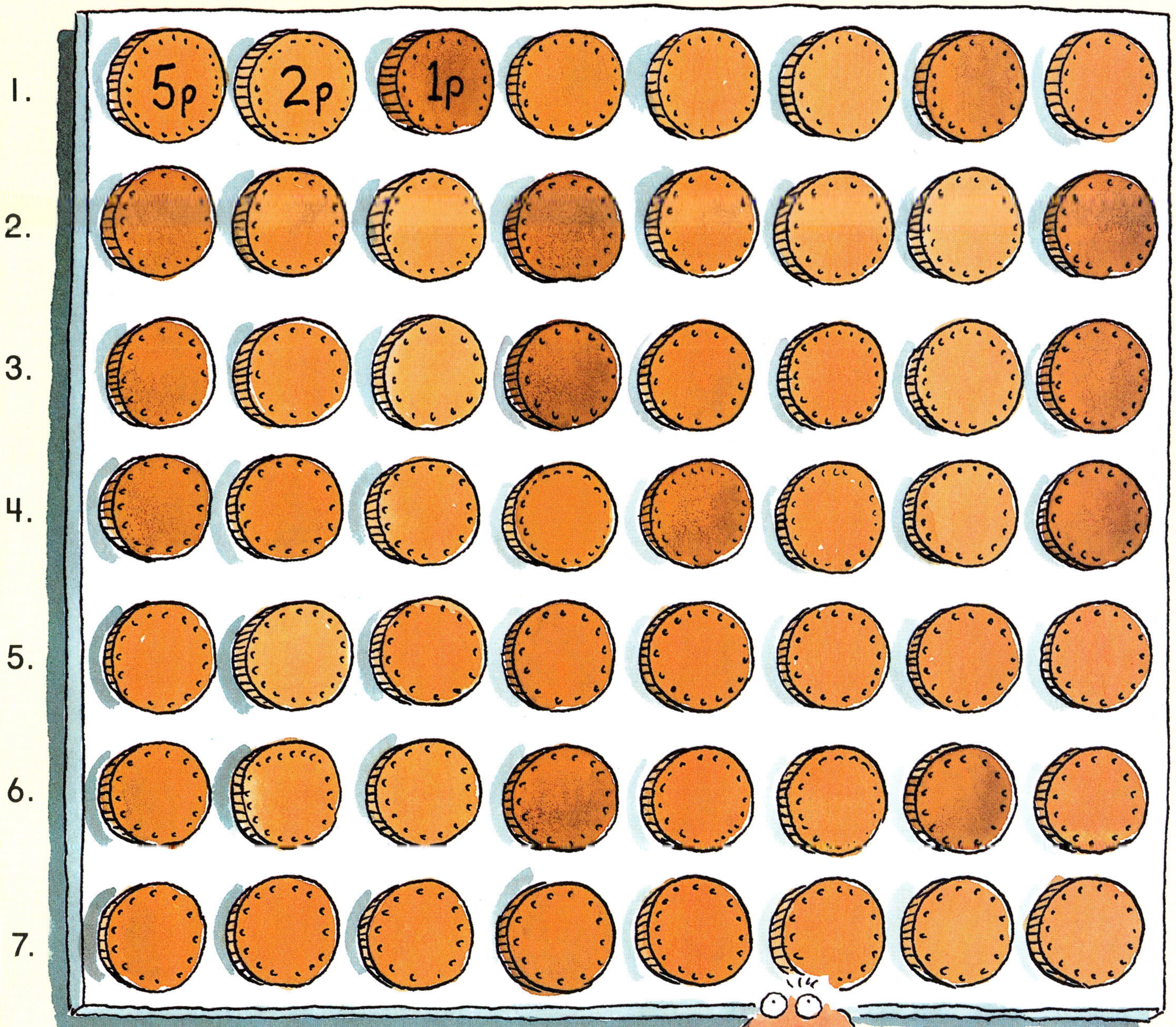

1. 5p 2p 1p

2.

3.

4.

5.

6.

7.

Supposing the lollipops went up to 10p.
How many ways could you pay 10p?
Write them down on a piece of paper.

Answers on page 32.

Vital statistics

Use a tape-measure to measure your family's heads, feet and hands.

Fill in the chart.

name	foot	hand	head
	cms	cms	cms
	cms	cms	cms
	cms	cms	cms
	cms	cms	cms
	cms	cms	cms
	cms	cms	cms

Who has the biggest head?

Who has the smallest foot?

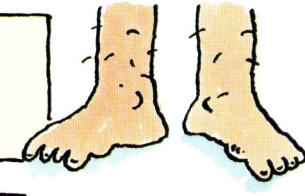

Does the person with the biggest hand have the biggest foot?

Does the person with the smallest head have the smallest hand?

Think of some more questions of your own.

Broken calculator

You need
A calculator

I only have these keys working: **3 4 + = ON/C**

Can you help me show as many numbers as possible on my display by pressing only those keys? You can press them as many times as you like!

Show how you made each number (put a cross if you can't).

1	2	3	4	5	6
x	x	press 3	press 4	x	3 + 3 =

I have done the first line. Can you do the rest?

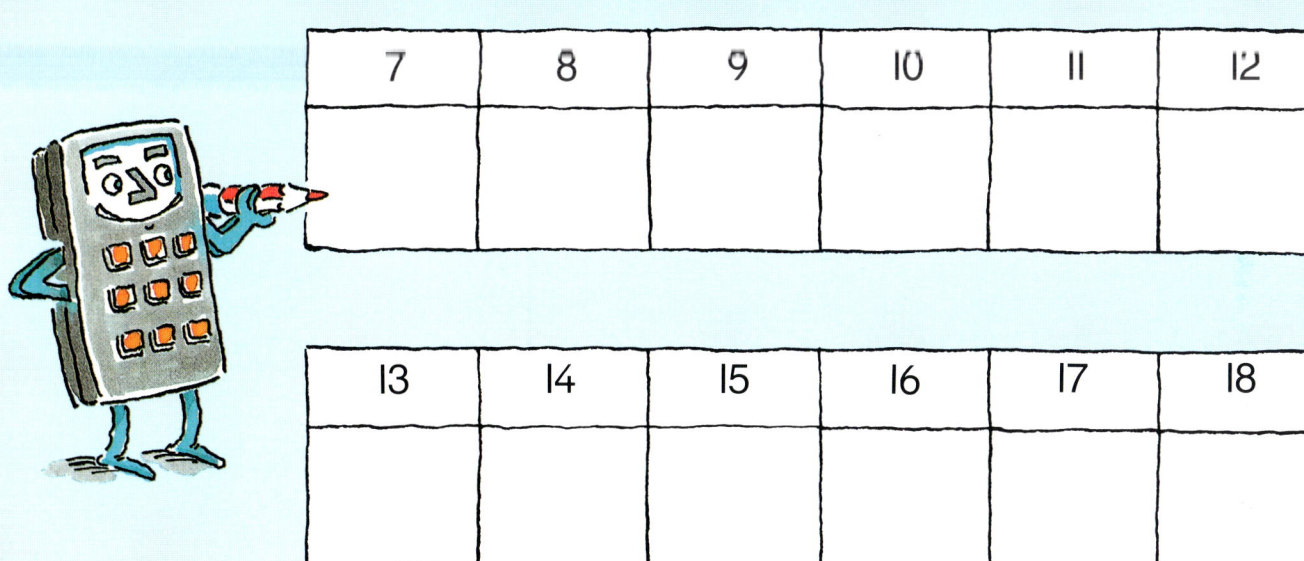

Answers on page 32.

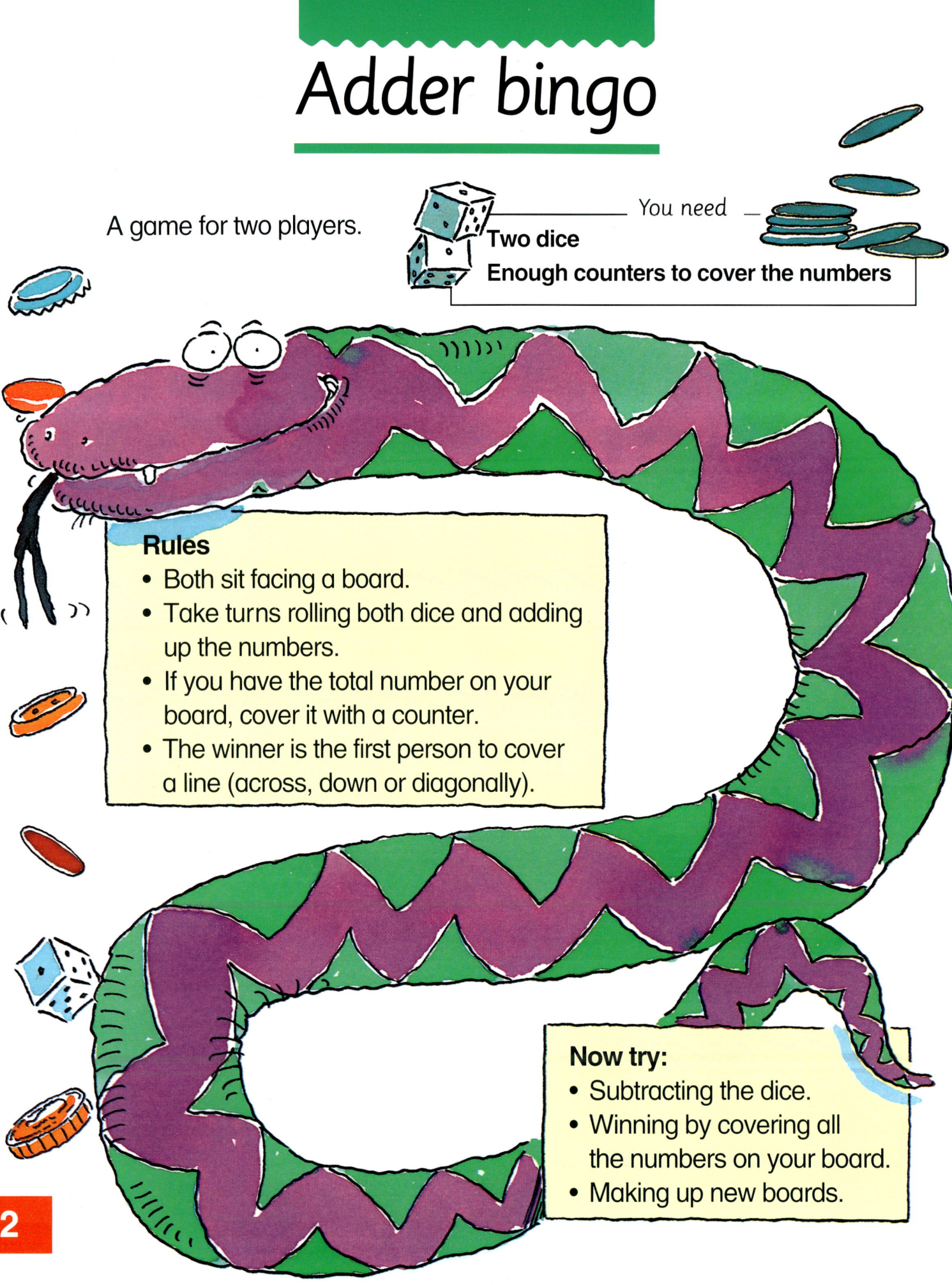

Adder bingo

A game for two players.

You need
Two dice
Enough counters to cover the numbers

Rules
- Both sit facing a board.
- Take turns rolling both dice and adding up the numbers.
- If you have the total number on your board, cover it with a counter.
- The winner is the first person to cover a line (across, down or diagonally).

Now try:
- Subtracting the dice.
- Winning by covering all the numbers on your board.
- Making up new boards.

Player B

9	7	6
5	7	8
6	4	5

4	10	7
5	6	5
7	8	6

Player A

New prices

What if all the 1p 2p and 5p coins disappeared?

Can you help the shop assistants change the prices by rounding them up or down to the nearest 10p?

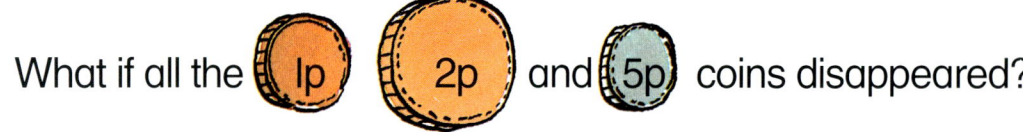

So 37p rounds up to 40p...

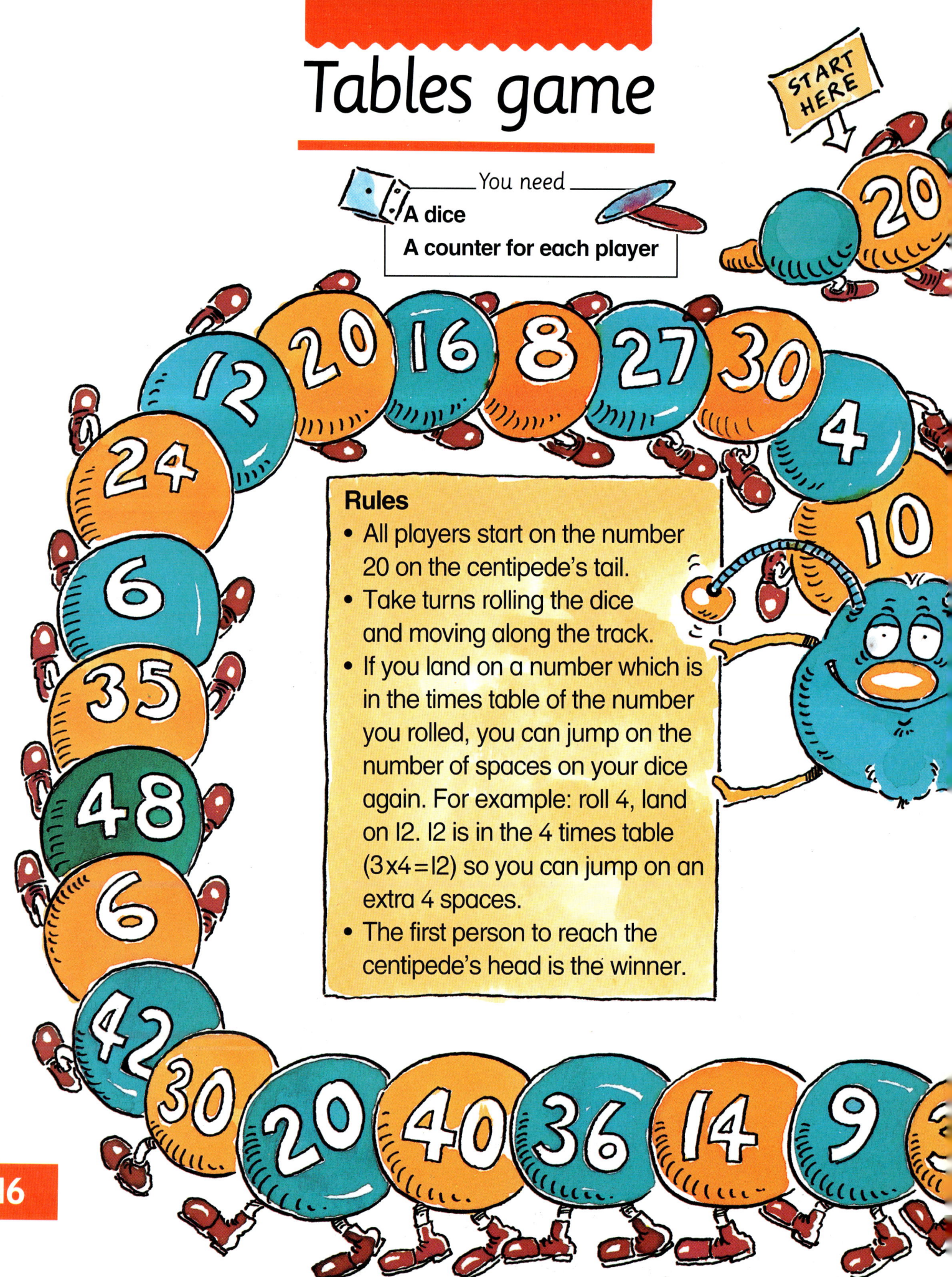

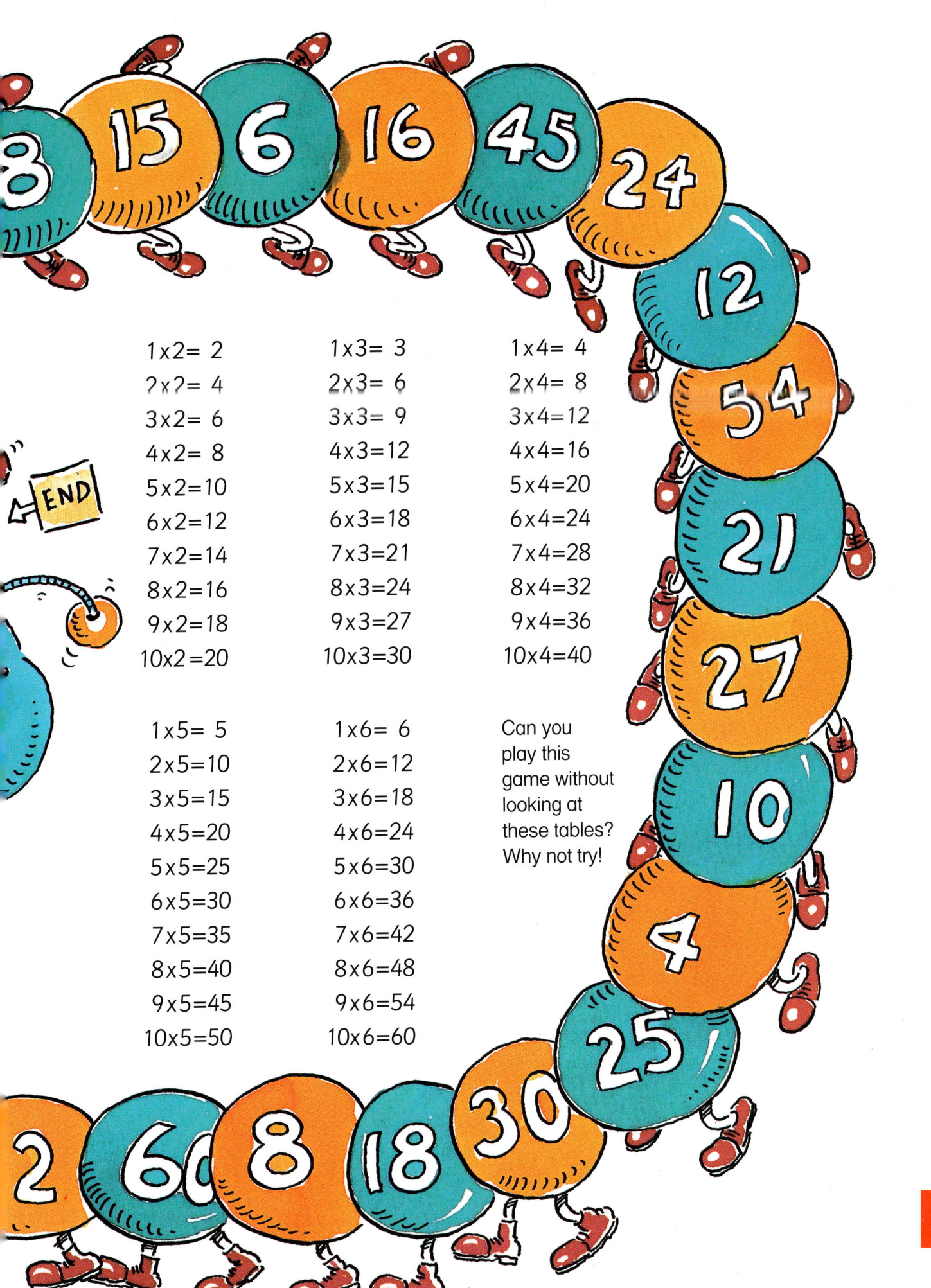

```
1 x 2 =  2      1 x 3 =  3      1 x 4 =  4
2 x 2 =  4      2 x 3 =  6      2 x 4 =  8
3 x 2 =  6      3 x 3 =  9      3 x 4 = 12
4 x 2 =  8      4 x 3 = 12      4 x 4 = 16
5 x 2 = 10      5 x 3 = 15      5 x 4 = 20
6 x 2 = 12      6 x 3 = 18      6 x 4 = 24
7 x 2 = 14      7 x 3 = 21      7 x 4 = 28
8 x 2 = 16      8 x 3 = 24      8 x 4 = 32
9 x 2 = 18      9 x 3 = 27      9 x 4 = 36
10 x 2 = 20     10 x 3 = 30     10 x 4 = 40

1 x 5 =  5      1 x 6 =  6
2 x 5 = 10      2 x 6 = 12
3 x 5 = 15      3 x 6 = 18
4 x 5 = 20      4 x 6 = 24
5 x 5 = 25      5 x 6 = 30
6 x 5 = 30      6 x 6 = 36
7 x 5 = 35      7 x 6 = 42
8 x 5 = 40      8 x 6 = 48
9 x 5 = 45      9 x 6 = 54
10 x 5 = 50     10 x 6 = 60
```

Can you play this game without looking at these tables? Why not try!

Maths factory

All the machines in the maths factory change numbers in some way (for example, adding on or taking away). See if you can find out what each machine does to the numbers and write it on the machine.

The first one has been done for you.

Answers on page 32.

19

Number trivia

Giant jumps

Clue
Giant jumps make a pattern! For example, look at the pattern made by jumping three tens from the number 2
2 12 22 32
– they all end in 2!

You need
A dice
A counter for each player

Rules
- Take it in turns to roll the dice and move along the track.
- If you land on a jump square, follow the giant jump instructions.
- The winner is the first player to reach or go past 100.

Now try this:

Look at each sum below. **Guess** whether the answer will be above zero or below zero. Then check your guess by doing the sum on a calculator. The first sum has been done for you.

	guess		check	
37 + 29	above 0	below 0	above 0	below 0
	✓		✓	

	guess		check	
99 − 33	above 0	below 0	above 0	below 0

	guess		check	
33 − 99	above 0	below 0	above 0	below 0

	guess		check	
77 − 91	above 0	below 0	above 0	below 0

	guess		check	
7 + 8	above 0	below 0	above 0	below 0

	guess		check	
253 − 353	above 0	below 0	above 0	below 0

Number square patterns

1	2	3	4		6	7	8	9	10
	12	13	14	15	16	17	18		20
21	22		24	25	26	27	28	29	
31	32	33	34	35	36	37	38	39	40
41	42	43				48	49	50
51	52	53	54	55	56	57	58		60
61	62		64	65	66	67	68	69	70
	72	73	74	75	76	77	78	79	80
	82	83	84	85	86	87	88	89	90
91	92	93	94	95	96	97	98		100

- Fill in the missing numbers.
- Colour in all the squares that end in a 5.

What happens? _____

- Colour in all the squares that end in a 0.

What happens? _____

Start from any corner and colour in all the squares on the diagonal.

smallest

Now try the other diagonal on a piece of paper. What difference do you notice?

- Now write the numbers in order from the smallest to the biggest.

- Look at how each column of numbers grows bigger or smaller one by one.

biggest

Which number would come next?

- Choose any small square of 4 numbers from the big square. Total each diagonal.

- Try with other small squares. Do the diagonals always total the same?

Number jumble

These numbers are all in the wrong order. They need to be placed in the right order before Tina can play her game.

Write the numbers in order from the smallest to the biggest. One of them has already been put in place for you.

Clues
- Cross out the numbers as you use them to save you getting mixed up.
- Use a pencil and a rubber – it's easy to miss a number out first time round.

Can you make up your own game with the ordered numbers?

Games and puzzles

Cross number

Across
1. 6+2
2. The first three numbers.
4. 5+6-1
5. 10÷2
6. 2x2
8. Half of one hundred.
9. 100-5

Down
2. 8+3
3. 100+100
6. 4x10
7. Three lots of five.

Maths word search

Look for:
zero
quarter
million
one
eleven
circle
ten
square

q	u	a	r	t	e	r	g
t	w	v	o	e	f	o	h
a	b	p	z	n	r	t	s
e	l	e	v	e	n	i	q
r	c	q	z	j	u	n	u
m	i	l	l	i	o	n	a
y	s	x	k	e	n	l	r
c	i	r	c	l	e	m	e

30

Multiplication Mapping

5 lots of 3 fingers

Make 15 fingers

Can you map each sum to the correct alien?

4 x 2

3 x 10

6 x 3

5 x 5

7 x 4

2 x 8

Answers

Pages 4 and 5 Feed the birds: 5, 3, 2, 1, $2\frac{1}{2}$, 4, $3\frac{1}{2}$, $2\frac{1}{4}$

Pages 6 and 7 Lollipop machine: 5p, 2p, 1p, 5p, 1p, 1p, 1p, 2p, 2p, 2p, 2p, 2p, 2p, 2p, 1p, 1p 2p, 2p, 1p, 1p, 1p, 1p, 2p, 1p, 1p, 1p, 1p, 1p, 1p, 1p, 1p, 1p, 1p, 1p, 1p.
(The reverse can also count if those are your rules. For example: 1p, 2p, 5p, as well as 5p, 2p, 1p.)

Pages 8 and 9 Broken calculator: All the numbers from 6 onwards can be made, using multiples of 3 and/c1 4.

Pages 16 and 17 Maths factory: Machine A doubles the number, Machine B subtracts, Machine C adds 1, Machine D adds 1, Machine E repeats the number or multiplies it by 11, Machine F halves the number, Machine G adds 100.

Pages 18 and 19 Number trivia: 1 ≥ 2 2. 10, 3. 40 ≤ 1 5. 20 6. 22 7. 12 8. 999 9. 51p 0. There isn't one (You can always add l to it.)

Page 30 Crossnumber: *Across:* 1) 2. 2) 123. 4) 10. 5) 5. 6) 4. 8) 50. 9) 95. *Down:* 2) 1. 3) 200. 6) 40. 7) 15.

Page 31 Multiplication mapping: 4 x 2 = 8; 3 x 10 = 30; 6 x 3 = 18; 5 x 5 = 25; 7 x 4 = 28; 2 x 8 = 16.

British Library Catalouging in Publication Data

Clarke, Shirley
 Headstart: 7-9 Number Skills (Headstart)
 I Title II Silsby. Barry III Series
 372.7

ISBN 1-86019-527-X

First published 1992

© 1992 Shirley Clarke and Barry Silsby

This edition published 1997 by Brockhampton Press, a member of Hodder Headline PLC Group
10 9 8 7 6 5 4 3 2 1
1999 1998 1997

All rights reserved. No part of this publication may be reproduced or transmitted in any form or by any means, electronic or mechanical, including photocopy, recording, or any information storage and retrieval system, without permission in writing from the publisher or under licence from the Copyright Licensing Agency Limited. Further details of such licences (for reprographic reproduction) may be obtained from the Copyright Licensing Agency Limited, of 90 Tottenham Court Road, London WIP 9HE.

Typeset by DP Press Ltd, St Julians, Sevenoaks, Kent TN15 0RX
Printed in India.